PRAY
for
EVERY DAY

By
REV. LAWRENCE G. LOVASIK, S.V.D.
Divine Word Missionary

NIHIL OBSTAT: Daniel V. Flynn, J.C.D., Censor Librorum
IMPRIMATUR: ✠ James P. Mahoney, D.D., Vicar General, Archdiocese of New York

Printed in India   ISBN 978-0-89942-381-4   CPSIA   December 2009   10 9 8 7 6 5 4 3 2 1   B/B

2

A PRAYER OF FAITH IN GOD

I BELIEVE in one God
in three Divine Persons.

I believe in You,
God the Father, Who made me
and all things in the world.

I believe in You,
God the Son, Who died
and rose from the dead to save me.

I believe in You,
God the Holy Spirit,
Who was sent by the Father
and the Son
to make me holy.

TO THE HOLY SPIRIT

HOLY SPIRIT, my God,
the Third Person
of the Blessed Trinity,
I love You.

You are the Love of God
the Father and the Son.

They sent You to the Church
to make it holy.

I thank You for the grace
You have given me
to make my soul beautiful
and to help me to be good.

Your grace made me a child of God;
it opened heaven to me.

Holy Spirit, live in my soul,
and take me to heaven someday.

5

6

TO MY GUARDIAN ANGEL

ANGEL of God,
my Guardian dear,
God's love for me
has sent you here.
Ever this day
be at my side,
to light and guard,
to rule and guide.

My dear Guardian Angel,
keep me from all danger
and lead me to heaven.

TO SAINT JOSEPH

GOOD Saint Joseph,
    I love you as the foster father of
    Jesus,
    as the holy husband of the Virgin
    Mary,
as the head of the Holy Family,
and as the patron of the whole Church.

Be my father and guide
    on my way to heaven.

Take care of me
    as you took care of Jesus.

Be the head of our family
    and lead us close to God.

Saint Joseph, give us peace
    and blessing from heaven
    and, above all, love.

TO JESUS IN THE HOLY EUCHARIST

JESUS, I love You
    in Holy Communion
    when You give me
    Your Body and Blood
    as Food for my soul.

Come to me, Jesus,
    and stay with me.

Jesus, bless our family.

Give us Your grace
    to help us to be good
    and stay away from evil.

May we receive You
    in Holy Communion
    every time we go to Holy Mass.

Jesus, be our best Friend
    and take us to heaven someday,
    where we shall always be with You.

Another Prayer for Thursdays

TO JESUS IN THE TABERNACLE

JESUS, I thank You
for staying in the tabernacle
day and night to be with me
and to hear my prayers
when I need Your help.

You are my best Friend.

I want to come to visit You often.

I want to show You how much I love You,
and to ask You to help me
and those I love.

O Sacrament most holy,
O Sacrament divine!

All praise and all thanksgiving
be every moment Thine!

TO JESUS OUR SAVIOR

JESUS, I thank You,
  for having suffered and died
  on the Cross
  to make up for my sins
  and to win grace for my soul.

I thank You for having opened
  heaven to me
  by Your death on the Cross.

Jesus, You are my Friend.

You showed how much You love me
  by dying on the Cross for me.

Without You I cannot save my soul.

As You gave Your life for me,
  may I always live my life for You.

Prayer for Saturdays

TO THE BLESSED VIRGIN MARY

BLESSED Virgin Mary,
Jesus gave you to me
as my Mother
when He was dying on the Cross.

I want to love you as Jesus did.

I pray to you in these words:

Hail Mary, full of grace!
The Lord is with thee;
blessed art thou among women,
and blessed is the fruit
of thy womb, Jesus.

Holy Mary, Mother of God,
pray for us sinners,
now and at the hour
of our death. Amen.

18

PRAYER TO THE INFANT JESUS

JESUS, Divine Infant, I thank You
for becoming a Child like me.

You were born of the Virgin Mary
so that You would be able
to suffer for me
and to save my soul.

You are God and yet You wanted
to be a Child like me
to help me to love You more.

Little Infant Jesus, I love You.
I give myself to You
as You gave Yourself to me.

Mother Mary, you loved Jesus so much.

Tell Him that I love Him
for coming to us as a Child to help us
and to take us to heaven.

Morning Prayer

THANK YOU, O God,
for this new day.

Help me in body and soul,
in my work and play.

Bless all I do or think or say.

Let me do everything to please You,
and to keep me from all danger and sin.

Evening Prayer

O GOD, I thank You
    for being good to me.

Forgive me for anything
    I have done
to displease You this day.
I am sorry!

Bless my father and mother,
    my brothers and sisters,
    all those I love,
    and the children of the whole world.

Thanks for the World

HEAVENLY FATHER, I thank You
for the life You gave me
and for all the things You do
to make me happy in this world.

I thank You for the stars and sky,
for hills and fields and lakes,
for flowers, trees and grass,
for birds and all the animals.

You made all these things.

Never let me forget Your love for me.

I give You all my love, and all that I do.

I want to be good to please You
as Your loving child.

Thank You, my dearest God,
for being my Father.

24

Thanks for My Country

LORD GOD, I give You thanks
    for letting me live
    in this great land,
    which is filled with good things.

Thank You for letting me be free
    to live in peace
    and to worship You without fear.

Take care of our President
    and let him be a good ruler.

Watch over our other leaders in government
    and help them to make just laws.

Help all the citizens of our country
    to follow Your holy Will
    and to live in love for each other
    and for You.

Thanks for My Family

I THANK YOU, my God,
for the loving family
and good home
You gave me.

I thank You for the love
of my mother and father,
my brothers and sisters.

I thank You for my daily food
and for the clothes and toys
and for the many good things
You give me at home.

Lord, bless our dear family
and give us Your grace
that we may live in peace and love.

Take us all to heaven someday
to be with You forever.

Thanks for My Teachers

LORD, my teachers work hard
    to help me learn
      many important things I have to know
    in my daily life.

Thank You for my teachers,
    and all who teach me about You.

Help me to study hard
    to please them and especially You.

Thanks for My Friends

J ESUS,
    I thank You
    for my
    friends.

You gave them to me
   to make my life happy.

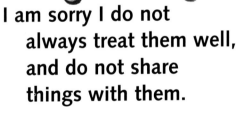

I am sorry I do not
    always treat them well,
    and do not share
    things with them.

I will try to love
   the friends
   You gave me.

Bless them, dear Lord,
    and help them
    to love You.

Thanks for Those Who Help Us

HEAVENLY FATHER, I thank You
for all the people
who help us:
doctors, nurses, police officers,
firefighters, and many working
people.

Bless those who are kind to me.

Reward them in heaven someday.

Thanks for Those Who Help Us Pray

DEAR LORD,
bless our Holy Father,
our Bishops and priests,
who take Your place among us.

They teach us Your truth,
take away our sins, and offer Holy Mass.

Help them in their work for the Church.

Bless all those who teach us
to know and love You.

Reward them in heaven.

Thanks for Each Day

DEAR Jesus, I thank You
for each day of my life.
It is a gift from You.

Help me to use it well
to serve You and the people
I meet each day.

Thank You for each birthday
that makes me think of Your love for me.

When my life on earth is over,
take me to heaven
to live with You forever.